ARC AND SEAM:
POEMS BY FAROUK GOWEDA

Translated by

Walid Abdallah and Andy Fogle

Finishing Line Press
Georgetown, Kentucky

ARC AND SEAM:
POEMS BY FAROUK GOWEDA

Copyright © 2022 by Andy Fogle
ISBN 978-1-64662-915-2 First Edition
All rights reserved under International and Pan-American Copyright Conventions. No part of this book may be reproduced in any manner whatsoever without written permission from the publisher, except in the case of brief quotations embodied in critical articles and reviews.

ACKNOWLEDGMENTS

Our thanks to the editors of, readers of, and fellow contributors to the following publications, where these co-translations first appeared:

ANMLY: "Forgetting," "Gouge," "This My Country No Longer My Country," "We May Meet," "Who Said Oil Is Worth More Than Blood?" and "Your Scent Still."
Chicago Quarterly Review: "One."
Image: "Egypt's Grief."
Los Angeles Review: "Love in a Time of Terrorism," "Our Martyrs," and "Rainy Night Blues."
Reunion: The Dallas Review: "Mirage," "Strangers' Cross," and "Travelers."
RHINO: "Cause" (Translation Prize).
Toyon Multilingual Journal of Literature and Art: "Blood Merchants" (Barbara Curiel Multilingual Award in Translation, Multilingual or Spanish-Language writing).

We would also like to give special thanks to Allison Grimaldi Donahue, associate translation editor at *ANMLY*, for her precise and insightful commentary on "Forgetting," "This My Country No Longer My Country," "Gouge," "We May Meet," "Your Scent Still," and "Who Said Oil Is Worth More Than Blood?"

Publisher: Leah Huete de Maines
Editor: Christen Kincaid
Cover Art: Norman J. Olson
Author Photos: Walid Abdallah and Andy Fogle
Cover Design: Elizabeth Maines McCleavy

Order online: www.finishinglinepress.com
also available on amazon.com

Author inquiries and mail orders:
Finishing Line Press
PO Box 1626
Georgetown, Kentucky 40324
USA

Table of Contents

Travelers 1

Who Said Oil Is Worth More Than Blood? 2

Egypt's Grief 7

Strangers' Cross 9

Mirage 10

This My Country No Longer My Country 11

Forgetting 14

Blood Merchants 15

Our Martyrs 16

Cause 21

Dreaming Disquiet 22

Every Letter 24

Love in a Time of Terrorism 25

The Life You Are 27

Gouge 28

Rainy Night Blues 30

Your Scent Still 31

We May Meet 32

One 33

Travelers

My youth? Long gone,
and the now-young
have slashed their veins.

Our heady days are ash,
the wilderness of our dreams
has vanished like a mirage,

night smashed our hope, and we
had to swallow all that.
That's destiny for you.

Why gather in the world
of yearning? Why not keep
us apart? Don't ask me

how we got lost;
we were mixed up back then,
living love one day,

missing it the next,
so don't blame me if I turn
our life into song: I live

in the poem's ever-stream.
Do you see the clump of days
left like flowers in the night?

Don't be like roses people
toss in the streets the way night
did us, destiny's playthings.

Despite the map of my wounds,
I got lost. Despite the gag
of the past, I'll sing on.

Who Said Oil Is Worth More Than Blood?

As long as we are ruled by madness, hounds
will devour fetuses still in their wombs,
mines will sprout in wheat fields, and even
the crossed light of morning will be eye-fire.

We'll see the young hanged, wronged
at the dawn prayer. It's an age witness
to a snarling pig fouling mosques.

When madness rules, there are white flowers
on the ruined branches, emptiness
in a child's eyes, no kindness, no faith, no
dignity held sacred. All fates futureless,

everything present worthless. As long as madness
rules, the children of Baghdad can only guess
why they wander hunger's thorns,

why they share the bread of death, why off
in the distance, American Indians
hover in the cold, why greed shouts them down,
every race crawling ghost-hearted.

Through blood-colored streets, between humiliation
and disbelief, crippled shadows creep,
and the madness-hounds howl in our minds.

We are on our way to death.

***

The children of Baghdad scream in the streets
as Hulagu's army pounds the city's doors
like an epidemic; his grandchildren roar
over the bodies of our young.

The wings of wild birds are blood rivers,
black claws claw eyes—all this cracks the silence.

The Tigris River remembers those days, so look
behind the curtain of history—how many
aggressors have passed through the centuries
of our land, and still we resist?

Hulagu will die, and the Iraqi children
will dance in front of Degla. We are not
to be hanged from all corners of Baghdad.

***

A river can be a weapon against injustice on the earth.
A palm can be a weapon against injustice.
A garden can be a weapon.

Among the water, in the silence
of tunnels, though we hate death,
for God and right we will set fire forever
to your refusal that Islam is holy.

Baghdad, raped by tyranny, your children
are raising flags. Where are the Arabs
and the white swords, wild horses, glorious families?

Some of them were condemned, some
fled shameful, some stripped and gave away
their clothes, and some are lined up in the devil's hall
to get their share of the spoils.

And people ask about a great nation's ruins,
but nothing remains of that shining empire
that spans from the ocean to the gulf.

***

Every calamity has its cause.

They sold the horses and traded in
the knights in the market of rhetoric:
Down with history! Long live hot air!

Death comes to the children of Baghdad
in the smallest toys, in the parks, in restaurants,
in the dust. Walls collapse on the procession of history,
shame upon civilization, shame from a thousand borders.

From the unknown, a missile charges,
"Where are the weapons of mass destruction?"

Will daylight come again after the virgin smile
has been erased, after planes block the sunrays,
and our dreams spurt suicidal blood?

By what law do you demolish our homes,
and flood fire upon a thousand minarets?

In Baghdad, days pass, from hunger to hunger,
thirst to thirst, under the gaze of the master
of the mansion, the thousand-masked face.
Will there never be an end to this nonsense?

The curtain rises: we are the beginning.

To starve people—is this honor?
"To prey upon supplicants"—that's the glorious slogan of victory?
To chase children from one house to another—the joy of tyranny.

These days, people have the right to humiliation, submission,

death in every atom, and the chronic question,
"Where are the weapons of mass destruction?"

***

The children of Baghdad are playing in schools:
a ball here, a ball there, a child here, a child there,
a pen here, a pen there, a mine here, a death there.
Among the fragments, the cactus.

There were children here yesterday,
fluttering like pigeons in open spaces.
One of these days, dawn might lighten the universe,
but for now the sun of justice is far below the horizon.

***

Despite sacrifice, there is a dark gluttony:
some are faithful, and some are sellouts.

Oh nation of Mohammad, my heart longs for Al Hussein.
Oh Baghdad, land of Caliph Rasheed,
oh castle of history, and once-glorious age,
the two moments between night and day are death and feast.

***

Among the martyrs' fragments,
the throne of the universe, shaken by a young voice.
The dark night leaves when a new day flows.

Oh land of Al Rasheed, don't lose hope, every tyranny ends:
a child adores Baghdad, holds a white notebook and flowers,
paper and poetry, some piasters from the last feast.

***

Behind his eyes, a tear that won't break
but flows like light deep in his heart: the picture
of his father who left one day and never returned.
The child embraces ashes, and stays a long time.

A thread of blood runs through his mouth;
his voice and shed blood are one.
His features washed out; all of this world is separation.

The child whispers, *I long for Baghdad's day.*
Who said oil is worth more than blood?

Don't ache, Baghdad, don't surrender.
Although there is dissent in this blind time,
there is, in the far horizon, a wave of visions.

Although the dream is distant, it rises. Rise,
and spread my bones in the Tigris River,
so daylight will one day rise over my funeral procession.

God is greater than the madness of death.
Who said oil is worth more than blood?

Egypt's Grief

Egypt, we left you in the nightfrost
where winter stormed your shaky frame
and Heaven learned to weep. I see
in your face the longing for shelter,
how you smile despite the scars, and the sun
seeps up through the night. Behind lashes,
the ruin of tears. For now, pride
and revolution hold back more.

Driven by the cold, lines of exiles
settle in emptiness. In this stingy age,
the young who covet crusts of bread
left long ago. Your blood is lost
among the cracked skulls of women and elders,
lost in whores' perfume, lost in a glass of wine.
The Arab nation can't blame us
for being sick of the drums of brotherhood.

Beloved invalid, what happened to awe?
Where are the colorful clothes,
and the perfume that filled all creation?
We fleeced it all, even vows and modesty,
left you jilted in the ditch of our ignorance.

O holy land that still and forever summons hope for the pilgrim
O rose through which we embrace grief
O love that we adore in purity as well as sin

When we are discarded by darkness,
you are the one whose mouth is bright.
Don't abandon your breathing voice.
Tomorrow's sky alive again with your scent
and I will feel your body rise once more.

Come to us, beloved,
in the tattered age of strays.
Come for us, inner haven,
in a time of tyrants.
I got used to crying as soon
as I started, and now I can't stop.
While a glass shatters, grief persists
and purity is a rarity,
but your beauty beams and hums, autumn
blazing on despite winter's windy on-come.

We faithful children witness flowing springs despite the frost,
the scents of yearning, and the perfume of blood.
Your people, Egypt, arc and seam the generations—
don't ask anyone else for reconstruction.

Don't look back, searching for what
you have given. Be mouth and eye and
voice as you always have since
the earth's first secret, and forgive
us, O temple of the soul, O black
delta soil, forgive us for God's sake.

Strangers' Cross

Yearning always led me
to project my vision onto you,
was a chanting fidelity,
was faith's hymn through long nights.
Yearning made me fall for you.

Days pass, and adoration swells.
I set my bags at your door
and said goodbye to travel and trouble,
set down all my sins,
forgave their world and its people.

Yearning taught me how to survive
and how to heed the inside.
Now my eyes long light.
Even as yearning made me suffer love,
I still burn deep down.

We promised things, and now we're strangers.
Love, I have nothing left, but I still believe
in promises. If we are to be no more, know,
know, that I am the one
whose love is beyond this vision.

Mirage

You are lamenting love that left one day
for the world of the impossible.

It was a dream, but is there anything
except illusion and make-believe anyway?

Our life is a summer cloud's thick shade.

You lament love's autumn folds,
and the division of all we shared.

Who said anything lasts? Hopes melt
and a sole question remains: Why enter my life

if dreams only turn to sand,
heat-haze blurring into heat-haze?

This My Country No Longer My Country

—an elegy for the martyred Egyptian immigrants who drowned on the coasts of Italy, Turkey, and Greece

All my life I have wondered: where is the face of my country?
Where are the palm trees, the warmth of the valley?
In the horizon only darkness, and the headsman's image: it never
    fades away.
It is part of our fate, between birth and resurrection.
I live in the call that raises palaces from gray hills.
I long for my beloved land's honor of both will and drive.
I long for children dancing like drops of dew in morning.
I long for days whose magic has faded, the bustle of horses, the
    joy of feasts.

I miss my old country.
We moved, and it moved.
In every bright star, an orphaned dream.
Every cloud a gown of grief.
In the horizon, flocks of leaving birds forego singing, become a
    swarm of locusts.
This country traded in its land, fragments of the whole,
    subdivided for the auction.
All that remains of the hustle of horses is sorrow.

Our history is full of glistening horses, but now I only see the
    headsman raping the valley, and a gang that twirls the blood
    from our eyes.
The day's cries subside, and the tombs are heavy with ancestors.
There is no light from a wandering star.
No longer a release dove's coo.
Sadness cackles past us, drops by without an appointment.
Something has broken in my eyes.

The times are fed up with the revolution I loved to the edge of madness.
When beauty is pimped, even the morning gets beaten.
The land is devoured by the fire of slavery.
Don't ask me about my country's tears during martyrdom, when agony hunts every acre.
In the pale distance, beyond the black mountains, I see black mountains.
I see waves breaking over our heads, feel gravel grit my skin in the wind, as the horizon's line is washed out.

I raise my frostbitten hands to flag down a passerby, and see it is my mother dressed in black.
We embrace, as if saying goodbye, and the sea heaves on with its corpses.
Up until the moment of death, I will still rise with a bright heart, knowing this is my daughter's face carved on my chest.
Farewell, mother—a sack of salt is all our food.
Give my shirt back to my mother, she saw what I couldn't see: the string between destiny and death, a hijacked homeland that threw me away.

I see from behind the borders a parade of the hungry chanting for their masters' protection, and death-crowds cheering around the hungry.
In the middle of this weeping life, seized in the call of longing, the times passed me by.
Remember the story of a hopeful lover who left his home for the promise of another country?

It turns out that country had nothing to offer, could only bow to the pimp.

My pulse is heavy, and all will be silent soon.
The mirror of birth and death is glass-dust, and in its grains I see the headsman and his gang.

And I see the river, and I see the valley, and I open my mouth for silence, for a country that is no more.

Forgetting

I carried all I had through the tangled night, blaming the road
that spurred me backward to green windows, witness

to the hunger of our bodies, witness to the underside
of forever. Alone now in the road's slow night,

I re-sense the first days' blush, the flash
of your hand in mine: how do you bear all that is past?

Such bluff inside my boast: I will forget you.
I try to move on, but a shadow slides along, chiding that folly.

Beside the road, pale light seeps into yellow tulips,
and I quicken for what is lost: youth, freedom, dreams.

Aimless, I stare at the ground until dizziness takes me.
Somewhere in the dust of these empty streets where we began:

the warmth of our hands. Somewhere in this dust
our savoring footsteps, somewhere my roving tears.

Like the endless road, my story is here and there at once.
Can I resist the *was* that beckons? Shall I continue alone?

As your memory strums the chord in my chest,
the threads of my journey unravel, unravel.

Blood Merchants

Asleep on their mistresses' chests, they profane the age of Al-Walid.
The dust of our age collects beneath the bed, mingles with a
 mother's sadness and a martyr's memory.
Blood-dregs stain the cup.
The ruins of perfume and the breath of young girls hover in the air.
The merchants toss the young with soiled rags and slave-bread, they
 sell poetry and build a new palace.
On all their routes, with all their victims, they use poetry.
Every day is its own auction.

With the hunger of all of Egypt, I am called to fight by giving
 people poetry.
Let me face and hold their pain.
Let me ask, Is there more of this?

Shall we drink the tears of the earth and burn the roses of good times?
Shall we smash Egypt's dreams and bury the newborn morning?
Maybe hawk the martyr's bones, laugh at a mother who has lost her
 son?
Let's pawn her very tears, discern the homelessness of the youth in the
 wandering lines of her palm.

One of their dreams lies gutted beneath roses, but there are more in
 the market.
We have profited much off Egypt's open hand, and there is more to
 make.
With the perfume of slaves, we can lull the young to tears, and keep
 the crippled crippled.
We'll entreat them to have patience, like one tending to a garden
 where we planted disillusionment.

The low-down know: when the wound becomes cheap, so does
 blood.
We know dregs darken the cup.

We know dust collects beneath the bed.
We know when there is nothing of value left, we write new
   poems.

Our Martyrs

Inside their tombs, our martyrs are whispering,
Oh God, we are coming back.

On land they are lifting their hands,
and their voices grow in the silence of the grave:
Oh God, we are coming back.

Stones fall, ashes rise, and their eyes beam,
Oh God, we are coming back.

Our martyrs stepped out of their coffins,
lined up and raised the shout:
Shame on you cowards.
Our home is sold, our nation
a herd of sheep, and you sleep.

Our martyrs travel to Al Aqsa Mosque,
they pray in the churches of Lebanon,
they wander the streets of Jerusalem,
they break into prisons in every land.

They rise from the ashes of the captive home
and preach on every corner of a beaten nation.

They call in the midst of massacres,
God is greater than this man-made world,
God is greater than this man-made world,
God is greater than this man-made world.

Our martyrs are approaching, their shouts echoing
on the walls of Beirut. They gather in the streets
to fight in darkness despite the pale light.

In homes bound by humiliation and madness, they call,
Oh God we are coming back.
One day our coffins will light all of Jerusalem.

They are coming back to break into the castle.

***

On every corner, they ask the cowards,
Why did you tolerate the wolf, sleeping
amidst sheep, a home as whole as the universe
auctioned off, overrun with rats?

Cowards who sold out our broken home,
our living ancestors, there you are
on the screen, drunk in the fuss,
walking Death, hypocrisy, and control,
we will rid our holy dead of you,
and of the irony of the age.

Oh God we are coming back.

Don't believe that people killed
in a battle for God are dead,
they are still alive in God.

***

Our martyrs, roaring on every corner of the land,
streams of them asking,
Oh living, what are you doing?

Every day you're double-crossed and slain
like sheep, surrendering your rights,
running like rats to the wolves,
leaving your people weeping

while you are prostrate before America's
dollars and the images on screen.

Rats in all sorts of compromising ways.

And in the mad laughter of calamity,
a nation is sold into collapse.

Two images collapse into one:

while kneeling,
your heads under their shoes,
and our Arab Jerusalem,
given to wolves by the drunken.

***

With Lebanon adrift in blood, and tyranny
on the prowl, our martyrs shout
from every corner, *Does honor
have a place? Where have the rebels
disappeared? Why have the sellouts fled?*

The silent, the forgetful, and the two-tongued
all keep their mouths shut.
If you ask, they give you official nonsense.
If you ask, you get a bullet in the eye.

***

When you march in the parade of commerce
you wind up sold. History shows traitors
no mercy. The flood washes
over all of you chasing death
with the ad-man chasing you
to sell you tomorrow in the slave market.

Our priests are oblivious in their seats,
drunk on the power of reign and rule.

Our people in prison-darkness. All of them asleep.

When do the sleeping awaken?
When the sleeping wake.

Cause

Innocence can't survive these times, so I come to love you
before the void. We dreamed of a haven for refugees,
shelter for birds, water for palms. We watched spring turn to ash,

the sun burn itself away, the river of wine become blood.
The edge of my own pride was both border and blade.
Just look at how my hand can close.

But your love is my shade and my Nile,
and the ragged path of hope is still a path.
Come—we still dream within weariness.

Come—any day's light is still daylight,
and at night the moon still beams.
Love, we are pure revelation.

Love threads every agony, kindles the lost.
Consider: if I pulled the shutters, and squandered the faith
that made me, would that grieving quell anguish?

Since our eyes are pale night, faint light, let's send fire
into the abyss, shout in the impossible silence,
and weave a new image of leave-taking.

Dreaming Disquiet

Waves pull me away.

Afraid of dark seas, I've waited
my whole life for daylight.

Is this the story of grief again?

I once followed my heart
to its bloody end, dove

into its depths, hit bottom.

I turned back, forsook yearning,
cast off all that pain.

*

Waves pull me away, maybe
to a new love. I learned

to love long ago, made it

all my life, as it is
life, how we forget

the pain of travel, how

we learn to with-
stand such wounds.

*

Waves draw me out
to the shore of dreams.

I once came to you

like a frightened child,
a dazed refugee, an elder

seeking tenderness in others' eyes.

On your shore, my love,
I wrote my poems with a lilt

to the hilt. I dreamt

of our future: a love-lit path
to a house far in the wild,

a young child,

a soft song that streams
beyond, beyond,

but dreams can sink like sand.

All you left me were the ruins
of memory, the fog of the past spent

on your shore, where my heart

wavered, and waved away.
And yet now I return.

*

I said I was done with the shore
where dreams shimmered and were

then buried in wet sand,

but waves heave on towards another and again.
In this heart, the strings are sounding.

Put your ear to my chest once more.

Every Letter

I'm a poet, still drawing songs
from bleeding gashes, tending
an altar of bliss amidst
oppression, still writing although

every letter is a risk,
squaring me in the stooges'
twisted sights. Then again,
how many take in even one

of these stray melodies?
You know they don't want to hear it.
Speak a word of soul to the soulless,
raise a hand against stiff profitlines,

and that hand will be taken out, pierced
by an arrow in the night
from an assassin of the regime
that looks like anyone.

Love in a Time of Terrorism

Where did you come from?
What land gave you your life?
The horizon is studded with pieces of fire.

Who said that the jasmine tree
blossoms in blood fields, its perfume
scattered among the slaughter?

Long ago, the morning faded from my eyes,
and the light was swallowed by the cosmos itself,
not the mere canopy of dark sky we know.

The road forked, and you and I
were two stars behind a cloud.
We orbit each other in the vast.

There is now a willow tree on the horizon,
and the singing of a broken nightingale
that touched the very atmosphere before its flight.

Where did you come from?

You are the last night. Before
our winter, the beaches were empty
and the waves dizzied with their whirling.

I can't believe blood is all that's left
after a lifetime of love and poems.
I can't believe that the end of homelands

is in the name of religion: murder, suicide,
severed limbs. I can't believe that hunger
is the day, that tyranny and chaos line every road.

Where did you come from?

At the ends of alleys, in the depths
of tunnels, your look is like a thread of light
through a cutting dust storm.

How long I thought love was chance,
victim of circumstance. But no: here,
in this ringing emptiness, love is a choice.

The Life You Are

And one day
they might ask
about me—

if your love
is what breathed
into me—

say yes. Say
you are the
daylight that

bid me see—
I lived so
long to live

my way towards
you—but it
was no life.

Gouge

Does your blood make the fool drunk?
Do the ignorant dance on your corpse?
Does a hungry child sleep on your forehead?

For the hungry child,
for the dancing ignorant,
for the drunken fool,

this sorrow is mute in witness,
despair brains us with a length of darkness,
and helplessness gets cruel.

Beauty stands and does not step
as blood explodes from its two cheeks,
and the shadow of a cry wanders the maze of sound.

A coward eats the mother's flesh,
her entrails scattered
in the midst of wolves.

O my heart and my hopelessness,
O cycle of futility where all is null,
O you who are drunk with the burning of blood,

O children homeless upon the earth—

My child, Arabism is still
in Egypt, despite the gore, despite
the gouging, Egypt is love. Is giving.

*

If Egypt were not my homeland,
I would plant my heart in its soil,

take the path of love like her birds,
become a flower in a garden,

make the perfume of time a necklace,
and weave my faith between her domes.

In this world cramped in agony,
when will we restore the soul of Egypt?

*

Dear Egypt, dear friends, don't leave Al Ka'ba
to the idols of rabid money or careless lust.
They're not long for this world,

and this web of light deserves better
than petty theft. It deserves better.

God sings in us that despite sorrow
we hold to the shrine of the merciful.

O you who are drunk with the burning of blood,
O you who lash this land with your rubber tongue,
There is no good in money without a look in the mirror.

Rainy Night Blues

The ceiling is bleeding,
the wall moans with rain, and that
is how I drown. Other nights,
this grief drives me to the narrow
places: tight streets, inky alleys,

potholes in forgotten lanes,
and that is how I am cornered.
In my face are specks of the past,
and all the evenings' ghosts
sleep in my eyes. Clothes don't hide torment,

or the chain at my wrist, shackle
since who knows when. That's how it's been
all my life, nothing in my house
but night-silence, with hope
a passing cloud that morphs and fades.

There is a package in the far
corner: inside is a prayer
from my father and a spell
from my mother's heart. Her prayers
were like any mother's for her child:

long health, deep content. No one
answered, but none of that rends
my mind like the broken cry of this
wounded nation, like the broken
cry of the innocent's dream.

Your Scent Still

Even if you became a night,
a pool of shadows,
I still know your light.

Even if I were lashed
and twirled by khamaseen,
your scent is still my breath.

In every space I am
a wanderer, and my heart sees
no space as home.

There is no solace for
this pain on the shore,
no surge of renewal

as when a mariner
returns to the sea, but I still
adore the light.

We May Meet

Do you think the spring would return
and reanimate March into smoother days?

O unknown lover, we too may break this separation
and make belief of these tears.

If the days sweep us clean, tomorrow we might meet
and the birds will flutter their blue against the sky's.

One

When you're gone, I'm all horizon cloud.
How far between point and panorama.

Singing the days away, I walk the stranger's road,
lost with dreams, wild with poems.

Hard times are our lot, fortune teaching us to fret and mourn.
Even if the world's winds crumble us, the song still carries

the composer's breathing light.
When you are away, I know it is

my heart that is away.
I breathe with you, my breath.

When you're gone, I ask questions
about absence, always on its way, as when apart,

I turn to you, as emanate, and as return.
What was here is now there

and that's how distance grows.
What words can I offer

to be whole again, to make
two faraway points one?

Why deny the pieces of me in pieces?
I am not whole on my own. Only in other do I gather.

I see my heart in all people, and all people in my heart.
I see you as the light of wanderers, the music that waxes and
    wanes.

If autumn sprawls, you are still the quick current inside spring
    flowers.
God, how I can feel you still, like the sun, from so far away.

Scattered by this life, on the shore of your eyes,
my pain fades in that vast space of sand, sea, and sky.

These miles and borders have nothing on faith,
and longing is immune to time's needling increments.

When you're gone, I miss my heart between your arms.
Let's get lost—when your eyes and mine align, the space between
    is home.

Farouk Goweda is a bestselling Egyptian poet, journalist, and playwright whose nearly 50 books have been widely influential in the Middle East. His work has been translated into English, French, Spanish, Chinese and Persian, and he has been awarded several national and international prizes.

Walid Abdallah is an Egyptian poet and author whose books include *Shout of Silence, Escape to the Realm of Imagination, My Heart-Oasis, and Male Domination* and *Female Emancipation*. He has been a visiting professor of English language and literature in Egypt, Saudi Arabia, Germany and the United States. His prize-winning co-translations with Andy Fogle of Farouk Goweda's poetry have previously appeared in *ANMLY, Image, RHINO, Reunion: Dallas Review,* and *Los Angeles Review*.

Andy Fogle has six chapbooks of poetry and a full-length called *Across from Now* (Grayson Books). Along with his co-translations with Walid Abdallah, his poetry, collages, and a variety of nonfiction have appeared in *Blackbird, Best New Poets 2018, Gargoyle, Parks and Points, Right Hand Pointing,* and elsewhere. His music can be found at fogle.bandcamp.com. He lives in upstate NY, teaching high school and working on a PhD in Education.

www.ingramcontent.com/pod-product-compliance
Lightning Source LLC
LaVergne TN
LVHW041559070426
835507LV00011B/1198